what about... history?

what about... history?

Brian Williams

Miles Kelly
PUBLISHING

First published in 2004 by Miles Kelly Publishing Ltd
Bardfield Centre, Great Bardfield Essex CM7 4SL

This edition printed in 2008 by Miles Kelly Publishing Ltd

4 6 8 10 9 7 5 3

British Library Cataloguing-in-Publication Data
A catalogue record for this book is available from the British Library

ISBN 978-1-84236-795-7

Printed in Thailand

Editorial Director Belinda Gallagher
Art Director Jo Brewer
Senior Editor Jenni Rainford
Assistant Editors Lucy Dowling, Teri Mort
Copy Editor Rosalind Beckman
Design Concept John Christopher
Volume Designers Jo Brewer, Michelle Cannatella
Picture Researcher Liberty Newton
Indexer Helen Snaith
Production Manager Elizabeth Brunwin
Reprographics Anthony Cambray, Stephan Davis, Liberty Newton, Ian Paulyn

www.mileskelly.net
info@mileskelly.net

www.factsforprojects.com

CONTENTS

Ancient Peoples

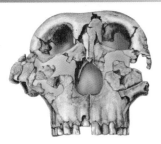

When was the earliest type of human discovered?
When did people first make tools?
How did fire change people's lives?
How did people hunt mammoths?
What are barrows?

Ancient Empires

Who made the first laws?
Who used chariots?
Where was Babylon?
What were the first towns like?
Who made the first writing?

Ancient Egypt

Who was Tutankhamun?
Why did the Egyptians build pyramids?
What gods did the Egyptians worship?
Why was the Nile so important to the Egyptians?
Who was the greatest warrior-king of Egypt?

Ancient China and India

When did the Indus civilization flourish?
Where was Mohenjo-Daro?
When did people first work with iron?
Why was the Great Wall of China built?
What are Chinese junks?

Ancient Greece

Who were the greatest Greek philosophers?
Why was Alexander so Great?
What was the Trojan War?
When was Crete the centre of a civilization?
What was the Parthenon?

Ancient Rome   18–19

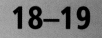

How did the Romans come to power?
When was Rome founded?
Why was the Roman army so powerful?
What was a villa?
What was a netman?
Why did the Romans build roads?

Ancient Britain   20–21

Who were the first Britons?
When was Stonehenge built?
What was a Celtic home like?
Why did ancient Britons build hillforts?
How did the Celts go to war?

After the Romans   22–23

Which queen fought the Romans?
What were the forts of the Saxon Shore?
How did Christianity reach Britain?
Where was the Battle of Clontarf?
Which English king led the fight against the Vikings?
Why were the Vikings so feared?

The Middle Ages   24–25

Who was Genghis Khan?
What were the Crusades?
What was feudalism?
Why did the Normans invade England?
Who signed Magna Carta?

Ancient America   26–27

Who built pyramids in America?
When did 180 men conquer an empire?
Why did some Native Americans make human sacrifices?
What was the Aztecs' favourite game?
Who was thought of as a god by the people he attacked?

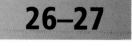

1400–1600 Age of Discovery

Who won the Battle of Agincourt?
Why was Columbus confused?
Who was the Virgin Queen?
Who sent the Armada to England?
Who destroyed England's monasteries?

1600–1800 Age of Revolution

What caused the English Civil War?
Where did Cook voyage?
When was London almost burnt down?
Who was Clive of India?
What was the Battle of Culloden?
Why did the Americans declare independence?

1800–1900 Empire and Industry

What was the Industrial Revolution?
Who was Napoleon Bonaparte?
Why did Napoleon fight at Waterloo?
Which war split the United States?
Where was Custer's last stand?

The Modern World

Why was the First World War the first modern war?
How did warfare develop after the First World War?
What was the Great Depression?
Why was the United Nations set up?
What is Communism?
What was the Cold War?

Human beings are related to primates (monkeys and apes), and our earliest ancestors, some four million years ago, were ape-like creatures that walked upright on two legs. As these human-apes evolved, they became less like apes and more like humans. Scientists have found evidence of this from studying bones and simple stone tools that have been found. Modern humans, our direct ancestors, appeared about 100,000 years ago.

When was the earliest type of human discovered?

In 1974, the almost-complete skeleton of an *Australopithecus* female was found in Ethiopia. Scientists called the ape-like human 'Lucy'. She was no taller than a ten-year-old girl, though she was about 40 when she died three million years ago. Preserved footprints found by Mary Leakey in Tanzania proved that *Australopithecus* walked upright, like modern humans.

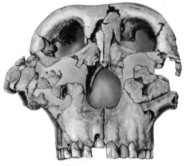

↑ *Skull of* Australopithecus, *the human-like ape that walked on two legs, leaving its hands free to hold sticks or stones.*

When did people first make tools?

More than two million years ago. Remains of prehistoric people found in East Africa are accompanied by pebbles and rocks that had been flaked to make sharp cutting edges. The first tool-users have been named

Homo habilis, which is Latin for 'handy man'. These early humans used stone tools to kill animals and to chop up meat and skins.

↑ *Stones were flaked by chipping away the edges and were made into cutting, scraping and chopping tools.*

➡ *Stone Age people lived in caves. They used fire for warmth and cooking. The flames also gave light for artists who painted animals on the cave walls.*

How did fire change people's lives?

People began to use fire to scare away wild animals, to keep themselves warm and to cook meat. The first people to use fire were *Homo erectus*, more than 500,000 years ago. They were skilful tool-makers. They learned how to rub sticks or strike sparks from a stone to start a fire, and then how to keep the fire burning. Without fire, people could not have survived in cold lands during the ice ages.

Steps towards **civilization**

Key **dates**

years ago

4 million	*Australopithecus.*
2 million	*Homo habilis*; stone tools.
1.5 million	*Homo erectus.*
500,000	Making fire.
120,000	Neanderthal people
100,000	*Homo sapiens.*
40,000	Painting and carving.*Homo sapiens sapiens*; widespread.
33,000	Neanderthals die out.

13,000	Making clay pottery.
11,000	Becoming farmers.
10,000	Farming begins; many tools are used.
7,000	First copper tools.
5,000	First bronze tools.
3,500	First iron tools.

➡ *Prehistoric flint mines were the best places for finding flint to make stone tools. Stone Age miners burrowed into the ground to gather the flint.*

↑ *Hunters used fire to frighten mammoths, driving them into a pit-trap, then killing them with wooden spears tipped with stone points.*

How did people hunt mammoths?

Prehistoric people worked together to hunt animals as big as mammoths, huge relatives of the modern elephant. Groups of hunters drove the mammoths towards boggy ground, cliffs or into pits dug by the hunters, making it easier for the hunters to kill them. A mammoth provided not only meat, but also fat, skin, ivory and bones. The skins were used as clothing to keep people warm. The ivory and bones were used to make tools and framework for huts. Other animals, such as reindeer, were also hunted for their hides, bones and antlers.

What are barrows?

Barrows are ancient burial places, usually an underground chamber made of wood or stone, covered with soil and turf. The word 'barrow' comes from an old English word meaning mound or hill. Other names you might see on a map are 'tumulus', 'tump' or 'how' – these are barrows too. There are as many as 40,000 barrows in England. Most barrows are sausage-shaped, with one end higher than the other, and date from Stone Age times. The largest are over 100 m long. Later Bronze Age and Iron Age barrows were often round or cone-shaped. Barrows were made by people who believed that the dead would need their possessions with them in an afterlife. At Sutton Hoo in Suffolk, England, a king of East Anglia was buried in a wooden ship beneath a barrow mound in AD 600s. This barrow was excavated by archaeologists in 1939.

↓ *Inside a barrow was a chamber in which the body of the dead person was placed, along with some of his belongings, such as weapons, clothing and jewellery.*

↓ *Discoveries of bones have enabled scientists to name the stages of human evolution, from* Homo habilis *to* Homo sapiens, *with smaller evolutionary changes in between each stage.*

← Homo habilis *means handy man. This era of humankind was so named because of the ability to wield tools at this time.*

Homo habilis   Homo erectus   Neanderthal man   Homo sapiens

Otzi the Iceman – murder victim?

In 1991, a frozen corpse was found in the mountains between Austria and Italy. Investigating scientists discovered that the corpse, named 'Otzi the Iceman', died some 5,300 years ago. He was between 25 and 40 years old, and it is believed that he was warmly dressed in animal skins padded with grass. He carried a bow and arrows, a copper axe, a backpack, a bag of charcoal, flints and dried fungus (to light a fire). He may have died of cold or exhaustion, but an arrow wound suggests he might have been the victim of a murder.

Once people started to farm and live in villages, the population in certain areas began to grow. Villages grew into towns, and towns into cities. Leaders of hunting bands became chiefs of villages and towns; the strongest chiefs became kings, ruling not just their own towns but also other settlements. These rulers created the world's first empires.

Who made the first laws?

The world's first law-making king was Hammurabi, sixth ruler of Babylon, who lived about 3,500 years ago. He drew up a set of laws to govern his citizens – for example regulating trade and taxes. Hammurabi's laws were introduced to protect the weak from being oppressed by the strong. The rulers of later empires, such as Assyria, followed his example.

Ashurbanipal was king of Assyria from 668 to 627 BC. He was a cruel soldier, but a lover of the arts, who built a grand palace at Nineveh.

Who used chariots?

Chariots were used by the first armies. A chariot was a wheeled vehicle, pulled by one or two horses. It was made of wood, with two big wheels, and was very fast. The Egyptians and the Hittites from Anatolia (present-day Turkey) fought one another on chariots. Chariots were also used by nobles for dashing around the countryside and hunting wild animals, such as antelope.

Where was Babylon?

Babylon was a great city between the rivers Tigris and Euphrates, in what is now Iraq. Civilization developed close to rivers, in fertile regions where farmers could trade with their neighbours. Two of the greatest kings of Babylon were the

Egyptian war chariots were drawn by a pair of horses. One man drove the chariot, the other fired a bow and arrow or hurled spears at the enemy.

Nebuchadnezzar II added new buildings to Babylon, including the Ishtar Gate, decorated with blue tiles and named in honour of the goddess Ishtar.

law-maker Hammurabi and the conqueror Nebuchadnezzar II, who built the Hanging Gardens of Babylon as a present for his wife, Amytis, to remind her of her mountain homeland. The gardens became one of the Seven Wonders of the World.

Wonders of the ancient world

The ancient Greeks and Romans listed the Seven Wonders of the World as the most remarkable things for travellers to see – mostly because of their size and beauty.

The Seven Wonders of the World

1. The Tomb of King Mausolus – at Halicarnassus.
2. The Pyramids at Giza – in Egypt.
3. The Hanging Gardens of Babylon.
4. The Lighthouse – at Alexandria.
5. The Statue of Zeus – at Olympia.
6. The Colossus – at Rhodes.
7. The Temple of Artemis – at Ephesus.

What were the first towns like?

The first towns were walled, and the houses were built of mud-brick. Two of the oldest towns we know about, because they were uncovered by archaeologists, are Jericho in Israel and Çatal Hüyük in southern Turkey. People lived in these towns over 10,000 years ago. All that remains of the towns now are ruins, but archaeologists have found pottery, textiles and fragments of walls, both plastered and painted.

Who made the first writing?

The earliest form of writing, dating from about 3,500 BC, comes from a region of Iraq, which in ancient times was called Sumeria. The Sumerians founded cities, such as Eridu, Uruk and Ur, all over Mesopotamia. They wrote on clay tablets with pointed tools, at first making picture-signs but then writing in symbols that represented sounds.

⬆ *Sumerian writing tools made wedge-shaped marks. The writing is called cuneiform, from the Greek word meaning 'wedge'.*

➡ *The houses in Çatal Hüyük had no outside-facing doorways. People entered through holes in the roof – this security system kept out unwanted enemies.*

Great **empires and rulers**

Egypt 3100 BC – united under King Menes (also known as Narmer).
Sumer (Mesopotamia) 4000–2000 BC – greatest ruler Sargon of Akkad.
Indus River Valley (Indian subcontinent) 2500–1500 BC – no rulers known.
Babylon 1800–500 BC – great kings Hammurabi and Nebuchadnezzar II.
China Shang kings from 1766 BC – first emperor Shih Huangdi 221 BC.
Ur (Mesopotamia) 2100 BC – at its strongest under King Ur-Nammu.
Minoan Crete 2000–1100 BC – named after legendary king Minos.
Mycenean (Greece and Turkey) 1600–1100 BC – greatest ruler Agamemnon.
Assyrian Empire about 800 BC – at its peak under the reign of the last great king Ashurbanipal in the 600s.
Persian Empire 521–486 BC – At its biggest under the Darius reign.

The ancient Egyptians lived beside the River Nile in Africa. In about 3100 BC, a king called Menes united two kingdoms, Upper and Lower Egypt, and established the first royal dynasty (ruling family). Later kings of Egypt were worshipped as gods. The Egyptians were great architects and artists, and developed an amazing system of picture-writing, known as hieroglyphics. Their empire lasted for almost 3,000 years.

⊙ *The gold funeral mask of Tutankhamun was one of the treasures found in his tomb, unseen for more than 3,000 years.*

Who was Tutankhamun?

Tutankhamun, pharaoh of Egypt, was only 18 when he died in 1351 BC. Later Egyptian kings were called pharaohs. His tomb, in the Valley of the Kings (not inside a pyramid) contained the most amazing treasures (because unlike other tombs it had not been robbed by thieves). Tutankhamun's tomb was opened by an archaeological team led by Howard Carter in 1922.

Why did the Egyptians build pyramids?

Pyramids were tombs built to guard the bodies of dead kings, along with their treasures. The first pyramid was built as a tomb for King Djoser of Egypt in the 2500s BC. This 'Step Pyramid', about 60 m high, was designed by Imhotep, the king's physician. Larger pyramids were built for later kings and some 80 pyramids still stand.

Royal burial chamber

Passages sealed after burial

Smooth facing stones

Entrance

Workers' escape passages

Mortuary temple

Life in ancient Egypt

The Egyptian soldier
Egyptian foot soldiers had to be very fit because they walked everywhere. Supplies were carried by donkeys. The soldiers fought with swords first made of copper, then bronze, and later (after about 1000 BC) iron. They also had daggers and wooden spears with metal points. Other favourite Egyptian weapons were clubs, axes, and bows and arrows. Many Egyptian boys learned to shoot bows while hunting ducks in the Nile marshes.

⊙ *An Egyptian soldier carried a long spear and shield.*

Key dates

before 5000 BC	First farm villages beside the Nile.
about 3000 BC	King Menes unites Upper and Lower Egypt.
2575–2130 BC	Old Kingdom – Great Pyramids.
1938–1600 BC	Middle Kingdom – wars with Nubians in south.
1539–1075 BC	New Kingdom – Egypt at its most powerful. Wars with Hittites and Sea Peoples. Ruled by Ramses II.
from 600 BC	Foreign rule – Egypt conquered by Persians, Greeks and Romans. Ruled by Queen Cleopatra.

What gods did the Egyptians worship?

The Egyptians had many gods. People worshipped local gods in their own city or region. The greatest local god was Amun, the Sun god Ra or Re. Other gods included the cat-headed Bast, Thoth, god of learning, Osiris, god of farming and civilized life, Isis, the mother-goddess, her son Horus, god of heaven, and Anubis, god of the dead.

◉ The Nile was Egypt's lifeline, a green strip of civilization next to desert on either bank. People used reed boats to sail up and down the busy river.

◉ Two of the three Great Pyramids at Giza are over 130 m high. These amazing feats of engineering were built in the 2600s BC, by thousands of slaves hauling blocks of stone.

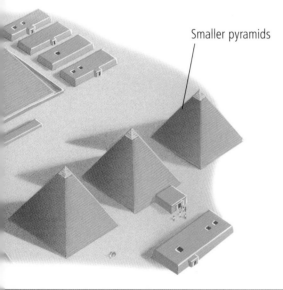

Smaller pyramids

Why was the Nile so important to the Egyptians?

The Nile is the longest river in Africa, and its waters made farming possible for the people of hot, dry Egypt. Every year the Nile floods, as snow melts in mountains to the south, raising the level of the water. As it floods, the river spreads fertile mud over the land, which enabled Egypt's farmers to grow plentiful crops. They dug irrigation ditches to carry the Nile water to their fields. The Egyptians also used some of the world's earliest boats, called 'feluccas' to sail up and down the Nile to travel between neighbouring farms and towns.

◉ Ramses II was a great warrior-king, whose soldiers fought to defend and enlarge Egypt's empire.

Who was the greatest warrior-king of Egypt?

Ramses II who reigned 1289–24 BC. Ramses led the Egyptian army into battle against the warmongering Hittite people, and in 1275, fought a great battle with them at Kadesh for control of Syria. Ramses built a huge temple at Abu Simbel beside the Nile. Outside this rock temple were huge statues of the great king. His temple was moved in the 1960s when the Aswan Dam flooded its original site.

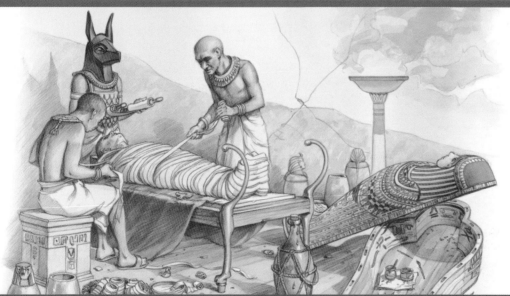

Making mummies

The word 'mummy' comes from the Persian word for 'tar', because the Persians wrongly thought the Egyptians preserved dead bodies in tar. In fact, the process took over a month and involved removing all the vital organs, except the heart, and drying the body in chemicals. The body was then stuffed with spices and linen, and wrapped in more linen. The aim was to preserve the body so that the spiritual parts of a person (known as ka and ba) would survive after death.

◉ The priest in charge of the mummification wore a jackal mask to represent Anubis, god of the dead.

Civilizations, with towns, agriculture, laws and flourishing trade, developed in several parts of the world at roughly the same time. As well as the great cities of Egypt and Mesopotamia, other civilizations arose in the Indian subcontinent and in China. Like the earlier ones, these civilizations were first developed alongside rivers.

When did the Indus civilization flourish?

Between 2500 and 1500 BC. It emerged along the Indus River in what is now Pakistan. The Indus Valley civilization was larger than Sumer or ancient Egypt. Why this prosperous civilization came to an end is a mystery, but floods and foreign invaders may have helped bring about its downfall.

⬆ The peoples of the Indus Valley lived as farmers and traders. Their two great cities were Harappa and Mohenjo-Daro.

⬇ The houses in Mohenjo-Daro were built around a central courtyard. The walls were made using mud-bricks that had been baked in a kiln. The houses all had a flat roof. The streets were straight and crossings were at a right angle, creating a grid system similar to that found in many modern cities.

Where was Mohenjo-Daro?

This was one of the two great cities in the ancient Indus Valley. The name Mohenjo-Daro means 'Mound of the Dead'. The city was set out in a neat grid pattern with 40,000 people living in houses of mud-brick with bathrooms linked to the city drains, and a large bathhouse – which may have been used for public bathing during religious ceremonies. The other major city of the Indus region was Harappa.

Inventive Chinese

⬇ The Chinese were very talented at devising water wheels turned by falling water and linked by other wheels and shafts to machinery.

⬆ The 'Heaven-Rumbling Thunderclap Fierce Fire Erupter' was a gunpowder-fired device that shot out shells of poisonous gas.

⬆ Acupuncture is a treatment still used in medicine today. It involves sticking needles into special points – as indicated on this diagram – on the bodies of people or animals.

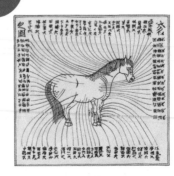

⬇ The first earthquake detector worked using a metal ball, which fell from the dragon's mouth at the top of the jar, into the toad's mouth – when even a distant quake occurred.

⬆ *The Great Wall was built mainly during the Qin dynasty (221–206 BC). Its total length was over 2,400 km.*

When did people first work with iron?

About 1500 BC, when the Hittites of the Near East began smelting iron ore (heating iron-bearing rock to extract the metal). People only had stone tools until around 7000 BC, when the Hittite people in Anatolia (present-day Turkey) started using copper. Later, people invented bronze (an alloy or mixture of copper and tin), but iron was harder, sharper and long-lasting.

➡ *The Zhou rulers, who ousted the last Shang king in 1122 BC, introduced iron tools and weapons to China.*

Why was the Great Wall of China built?

To protect the Chinese empire from foreign invaders. China had built a great civilization, beginning with the Shang rulers (about 1500–1027 BC). The first ruler to control all China was the emperor Shih Huang-di (221 BC). His greatest project was the Great Wall – not only did it keep out barbarians from the steppes of Central Asia. it also kept in the Chinese people.

What are Chinese junks?

Chinese sailing ships, which had sails made of woven matting, which looked like 'venetian' window blinds and were simple to operate. Some junks had five or more masts and were bigger than any western ships. For steering, Chinese sailors used the stern rudder – long before it was known in Europe. Chinese ships sailed as far as Arabia, East Africa and Indonesia, and it is likely that Chinese explorers investigated the north coast of Australia. Such voyages increased trade and made the emperor feel more powerful, but the Chinese did not set up permanent trading posts in foreign countries, as European explorers did from the late 1400s. Fleets of junks were used by pirates to ambush merchant ships in the South China Sea and the Indian Ocean.

⬇ *Chinese pirates such as Ching-Chi-Ling and Shap-'ng-tsai sailed in a fleet of junks. The South China Sea was perfect for pirates with its many small islands, swamps and narrow channels, in which ships could hide.*

⬇ *The Chinese invented mechanical clocks, such as this one – the 'Cosmic Engine' – built at Khaifeng in AD 1090.*

Important **inventions**

The Chinese produced an amazing array of inventions in science and technology.

Horse harness – Breast strap that did not choke a horse when pulling a cart.
Wheelbarrow – Some even had sails.
Acupuncture – System of medical treatment.
Paper – Invented in AD 105, and kept from the rest of the world for centuries. The Chinese were also the first to print on paper.
Abacus – For doing sums.
Stern rudder – For steering ships.

Seismograph – For detecting the direction of earthquakes.
Magnetic compass – Using a naturally magnetic stone called a lodestone.
Paddleboat – For water travel.
Watertight compartments – In ships.
Flame-throwers and gunpowder rockets – Weapons for use in war.
Umbrella – For use as a sunshade as well as for keeping off water.
Waterwheels – For driving machinery.

Greek civilization grew out of the earlier cultures of Minoan Cretians and the Myceneans – a race of people who lived in what became Greece. By about 800 BC, the ideas of Greek scholars started to spread throughout the ancient world. Ancient Greece was divided into small, self-governing city-states – the most powerful of which were Athens and Sparta.

Who were the greatest Greek philosophers?

Socrates, Plato and Aristotle – their ideas have influenced people over the last 2,400 years. First came Socrates (470–399 BC), who taught the importance of truth and virtue – he was forced to kill himself by his enemies. His friend and pupil Plato (427–347 BC), founded a school, the Academy in Athens. Aristotle (384–322 BC) was a student at the Academy and later also started a school, the Lyceum in Athens.

Aristotle came from northern Greece. He wrote about science, politics, art and religion.

Why was Alexander so Great?

Alexander conquered a vast empire and became ruler of Macedonia, in northern Greece, in 336 BC. He founded cities such as Alexandria in Egypt. Alexander had ferocious energy: after defeating the Persians he set out to conquer India. He would have gone on marching across India had his exhausted soldiers not begged him to turn back. Alexander died in 323 BC, aged 32.

Alexander the Great on his favourite horse, Bucephalus. He led his soldiers from Greece to India, and created a vast empire in just nine years.

What was the Trojan War?

The Trojan War was a ten-year war and the story is told by Greek poet Homer in his poem, the *Iliad*. Mainland Greece was dominated by warriors called the Mycenaeans from 1600–1100 BC. Homer's poem tells how the Myceneans destroyed Troy, a fortress-city in the region known as Asia Minor, about 1,200 years ago. The Greek army tricked their way into Troy, pretending to give up the siege and head home. Instead they hid soldiers inside a wooden horse, which the Trojans then took into their city. The Greeks clambered out at night and opened the gates to their army, winning the war.

Greek hoplites (foot soldiers) wore crested helmets and carried a long spear.

The glorious Greeks

The ancient Greeks
While some ancient Greeks were scholars, writers, thinkers and scientists, most Greeks were farmers, fishermen or slaves. Greek colonists settled all around the Mediterranean lands and Greek philosophy, religion, art and science formed the bedrock of western culture.

Greeks were excellent doctors, studying the human body closely to see how it worked. In the Roman world, almost all the best doctors were Greek.

The Greeks loved going to the theatre. Plays were staged in open-air amphitheatres – bowl-shaped arenas located on hillsides.

Plays were either comedies or tragedies, the two were never mixed. The actors wore masks to help the audience identify their characters.

The sculpture of Athena was more than 12 m tall and made of gold and ivory

When was Crete the centre of a civilization?

Between about 3000 and 1100 BC. This period of Greek civilization is known as Minoan, after a legendary Cretian king named Minos. The remains of the royal Palace of Knossos in Crete show what a rich culture once existed there, until destroyed (perhaps by an earthquake) in the 1400s BC. The palace was rediscovered in 1899 by British archaeologist Arthur Evans in 1899.

⬆ The Parthenon was badly damaged in 1687 when in Turkish hands. The temple was once decorated with painted figures and friezes. Made from beautiful white marble, it is one of the best examples of Greek architecture.

⬅ According to legend, the Greeks had to send seven girls and seven boys to Crete as sacrifices to a bull-headed monster called the Minotaur.

What was the Parthenon?

The Parthenon was the most splendid temple in Athens, which was the leading city-state in ancient Greece. During the 400s BC, the Athenians built temples and shrines to the gods on a hill called the Acropolis. The Parthenon was more than 70 m long and about 18 m high, and was built to house a magnificent statue of Athena, goddess of wisdom and guardian of Athens.

Greek pottery and artists
Greek art was at its finest during the 'Classical' period, about 400 BC. The Greek artists loved to show human bodies naturally, in statues and in pictures on pottery. Everyday pots were used for storing oil, wine and foods, but the finest pots were precious ornaments.

⬅ Pots were made in two main styles, with figures painted in red or black. They were often decorated with scenes from Greek mythology and history.

Key **dates**

500s BC	Greeks invent democracy.
490–431 BC	Greeks defeat Persians.
460–429 BC	Golden age of Athens under Pericles.
438 BC	Parthenon temple in Athens completed.
336 BC	Alexander becomes ruler of Macedonia.

⬅ Coins were first used by the Lydians (who lived in what is now Turkey) some time before 600 BC. The Greeks quickly adopted the use of coins for shopping and business. This one shows the head of Alexander.

The Roman Empire was the greatest the world had so far seen. By the first century AD, Roman rule extended over much of Europe, North Africa and the Near East. The Romans took their way of life and government wherever they went. They used their skills of developing central heating and running water and introduced their food and their language (Latin) to each country they conquered.

How did the Romans come to power?

The Romans were originally farmers from central Italy who rose to power by fighting their neighbours. They developed the city of Rome, erecting grand buildings and temples and eventually ruling all Italy. After conquering Greece, the Romans adopted many Greek customs and gods. Originally a republic, Rome became an empire in 27 BC, under the rule of Augustus.

⬆ *Coin of the first Christian emperor of Rome – Constantine the Great (AD 275–337).*

When was Rome founded?

According to legend, Rome was founded by Romulus and Remus in 753 BC. The Romans enjoyed the story, but actually Rome grew up from a cluster of tribal villages on seven hills beside the River Tiber. It was first ruled by kings, but became a republic in 509 BC when the last king of Rome was driven out. Roman society was divided into citizens and non-citizens, or slaves, who did all the heaviest work.

⬅ *Slaves might have been servants, miners, farmworkers, artists or even teachers.*

Why was the Roman army so powerful?

The Roman army was well trained and better disciplined than the enemies it faced. The best Roman units were the legions of about 5,000 foot-soldiers, who went into battle throwing spears and then rushed in behind their shields using short, stabbing swords. Roman soldiers were trained to march all day, build roads and forts, and swim rivers. Roman officers were usually politicians.

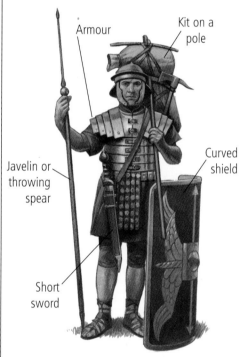

Armour

Kit on a pole

Javelin or throwing spear

Curved shield

Short sword

⬆ *A Roman soldier would march holding his javelin, sword and shield. His kit, tools and rations were tied to a pole over his shoulder.*

Rome wasn't built **in a day**

Key **dates**

c. 753 BC	Rome is founded.
509 BC	King Tarquin is driven out and Rome becomes a republic.
200s BC	Romans defeat Carthage (a rival state in North Africa).
146 BC	Romans take control of Greece, and adopt the Greek faith for their own.
49 BC	Julius Caesar rules as dictator in Rome.
27 BC	End of Roman Republic and start of Roman Empire.
AD 98–117	Roman Empire at its greatest under Emperor Trajan.
AD 286	Roman Empire divided into Eastern and Western empires.
AD 476	End of Western empire. Eastern empire continues as Byzantium.

⬆ *At its greatest, the Roman Empire ran from Britain in the west, as far as Africa in the south and Babylon in the east. The black lines on this diagram show the roads that the Romans built.*

What was a villa?

The Roman villa was a country house of a farm-estate, which produced grain, wine, meat, fruit and vegetables for the local people. Some villas were grand houses, with painted walls, baths and underfloor hot-air central heating. Rich Romans built themselves country and seaside villas as holiday homes.

⬆ A Roman villa was a working farm. The family lived in the main house. The farm workers lived in smaller buildings on the farm.

➡ Soldiers did the digging and stone-laying. Most Roman roads were straight, paved with stones and cambered (sloped) so that rainwater drained off.

⬆ Gladiators would fight in an arena filled with thousands of spectators. The netman would try to entangle his opponent in the net.

What was a netman?

A Roman gladiator, trained to fight in the arena. Roman rulers staged lavish and often bloodthirsty entertainments to keep the people amused. Gladiators fought one another or wild animals. There were various types of gladiator – the netman wore hardly any armour, and his weapons were a net and a trident (three-pointed spear).

Why did the Romans build roads?

Roman roads were built by the army to make sure that troops on foot and supplies in wagons pulled by oxen and horses could be moved quickly around the Empire. The Romans were excellent engineers and surveyed the route for a new road with great care, ensuring that the roads they built linked all parts of their vast empire to Rome. They also developed concrete, which was used in road building. Roman roads were built to last and many can still be seen today.

⬅ Wealthy Romans liked to feast. Often at banquets people would purposely make themselves sick, just so they could eat more!

Caligula the crazy

The Roman emperor Caligula spent the family fortune in a year, banished or murdered almost all his relatives, and executed anyone he disliked. He even tried to make his favourite horse a consul (an important official).

➡ When Caligula declared himself a god in AD 41, the army had him murdered.

Most famous **Romans**

Julius Caesar (c. 100–44 BC) – General, almost became king but was murdered.

Augustus (63 BC–AD 14) – Winner of civil wars, first emperor, had a month named after him.

Mark Antony (c. 83–30 BC) – Soldier, fell in love with Cleopatra, Queen of Egypt.

Hadrian (AD 76–138) – Soldier and emperor, famous for his wall in north Britain.

Nero (AD 37–68) – During his reign the city of Rome burnt down.

The prehistory of Britain began when the British Isles were joined to the rest of Europe by land, and when the climate was very different. In warm spells, much of southern Britain enjoyed a near-tropical climate. Most of the land was covered by snow and ice during the Ice Age. As people arrived in waves, they settled and began altering the wild landscape.

⬆ *The first people to settle in the British Isles lived by hunting and fishing, and by gathering wild plants and fruits. They made tools from stone and bone.*

Who were the first Britons?

The first people to live in Britain were *Homo erectus* people, an early type of human, who reached Britain by walking across what is now the English Channel. After the Ice Age, a 'bridge' of dry land linked Britain to mainland Europe. People started to settle in Britain about 500,000 years ago. The first 'modern' people arrived about 30,000 years ago.

When was Stonehenge built?

Stonehenge, a group of ancient stones in Wiltshire, England, was built in three stages, beginning about 3100 BC. Some of the stones, called bluestones, were brought from Wales, a distance of 385 km. The last stages were completed about 1300 BC.

Stonehenge was almost certainly built for ceremonial reasons, where religious rituals could be held. People also used the circle of stones to help them fix dates by studying the Sun and stars.

⬇ *Building Stonehenge, using muscle power alone, was an immense undertaking. The stones form England's most famous ancient monument.*

Ancient, ancient **Britain**

Key **dates**

years ago

500,000	First people settle in Britain.
230,000	Neanderthal people in Britain. People make flint tools and weapons.
30,000	First modern humans reach Britain from mainland Europe.
15,000	Ice sheets cover much of Britain during the Ice Age.
6500 BC	Sea level rises, cutting off Britain from mainland Europe.
5000 BC	Hunters mark out tribal territories.
4000 BC	Farming people reach Britain in boats from Europe.
3100 BC	First stage of Stonehenge work.
2500 BC	'Beaker People' skilled in metalworking arrive from Europe.
750 BC	Iron Age begins in Britain.
500 BC	Celts begin settling in Britain.
55 BC	Julius Caesar makes first Roman expedition to Britain.
AD 43	Romans begin their invasion and conquest of Britain.

⬇ *Smiths melted tin and copper to make bronze. The molten metal was poured into moulds to make items such as knives, swords and mirrors.*

Round-houses were home to the Celts living in Bronze Age Britain. The Celts kept their cattle and sheep in pens beside the house. The biggest round houses were up to 12 m high and 13 m wide, large enough for several families to occupy.

Why did ancient Britons build hillforts?

To make it harder for enemies, such as the Celts, to attack. The Celtic family of peoples lived across large areas of Europe, from Spain to Turkey, and reached Britain around 500 BC. They were warlike and quarrelsome, and often fought one another. The forts built by the ancient Britons had massive earth ramparts and wooden palisades as protection against any attacks. However, hilltop forts were insufficient to protect people from the invading Romans in AD 43.

What was a Celtic home like?

The Celts were farmers and their homes were round houses, as big as 10 m across, with room for several families. The roof was made of timber, covered with thatch. The walls were made of woven branches (wattle) plastered with mud and animal dung. On a central hearth burnt a fire over which people cooked food in large iron pots. It was dark and smoky inside because there were no windows and no chimney to let out smoke from the fire.

How did the Celts go to war?

The Celts wore very little armour when they went to war. Some men even fought naked. Most Celtic warriors were taller than many Europeans, which helped intimidate the enemy. They dashed into battle in chariots, dismounting to fight. Warriors shouted and blew horns and trumpets as they went into battle. Afterwards, the survivors would boast of their bravery in songs and poems.

A Celtic warrior, with spiky hair and colourful trousers, armed with sword and shield was a fearsome enemy to go into battle against.

Amazing **facts**

- Most of ancient Britain was covered with thick forest. People cut down trees to use the wood for fuel and building. Most of the ancient woodland was destroyed.

- As many as 50 people could be buried in one Stone Age tomb, called a barrow.

- A henge was a circle of posts, made from stone or wood.

- The Celts took pride in their appearance. They had tattoos, spiky hair and enjoyed wearing jewellery.

Polished metal mirrors, such as this bronze one were used before glass became widely available. Celts favoured this swirling style of decoration.

Metal bracelets and neck ornaments, called torcs, were worn by both men and women.

The people of ancient Britain made pots from clay, incised (cut into) with decorative patterns.

The Romans brought peace and prosperity to Britain. However, Britain was always on the fringe of the Roman Empire, and when the Romans withdrew their troops to help defend Rome itself, Britain was defenceless against attacks from across the sea. Waves of new invaders, such as Saxons and Vikings, arrived and over the years settled to become the English.

➡ *When the Roman army withdrew, many Saxons landed in Britain, seeking land to farm as well as plunder, because their own lands had become overcrowded.*

Which queen fought the Romans?

Boudicca (sometimes called Boadicea), who was queen of a tribe called the Iceni. She and her people lived in what is now East Anglia. When the Romans invaded Britain in AD 43, they quickly conquered the south of the country. In AD 60–61, however, the Iceni rose in revolt against the Romans. The Iceni destroyed London, Colchester and St. Albans, but then were defeated by the Romans. More than 80,000 Britons were killed. Rather than be captured and taken to Rome, Boudicca killed herself.

⬇ *Boudicca led a revolt following ill-treatment by Roman officials.*

What were the forts of the Saxon Shore?

The 'forts of the Saxon Shore' were built to guard the southern coast of Britain and keep out invaders. Until the early 400s when the Roman empire started to crumble, the Romans ruled Britain as far north as Hadrian's Wall. When Britain was raided by Saxons and other Germanic peoples, from mostly Denmark and northern Germany, the forts were not enough to keep out the invaders. By AD 410, the Roman army had left the Britons to defend themselves.

Early British **History**

The legend of King Arthur

When the Saxons and other invaders moved into Roman Britain, a British leader fought back. He became known in legend as King Arthur. Nothing is known of him for certain; all we have are stories about him. He may have led the Britons in a battle at a place called Mount Badon. The legends tell of a noble king, possessor of a magical sword Excalibur, who lived in a palace called Camelot, and gathered around him a group of knights – the Knights of the Round Table. As well as fighting evil enemies, the knights pursue the quest for the Holy Grail, the cup used by Christ at the Last Supper.

⬆ *Vikings founded settlements in northern and eastern England, and in Ireland.*

⬅ *The dying King Arthur ordered his sword to be thrown into the lake – and from the water, a mysterious hand caught it.*

How did Christianity reach Britain?

The Romans brought Christianity to Britain. Celtic monks founded monasteries and took Christianity to Scotland and northern England. When Roman rule collapsed, Christian Britons in the south fled to escape the pagan (those who believed in many gods) Saxons. In AD 597, the Pope in Rome sent Augustine to teach the Saxons (the 'English') about Christianity. Augustine converted King Ethelbert of Kent, and founded a church at Canterbury.

⬆ *This mosaic of Jesus from a Roman villa in Dorset was made in the AD 300s. It shows that the people who lived there were Christians.*

Where was the Battle of Clontarf?

This was a battle fought in Ireland in 1014, between the Irish high king Brian Boru and the Vikings. Viking raiders had made Dublin one of their key bases in the British Isles. In the battle, the Irish king was killed but his army won and ended Viking power in Ireland.

Which English king led the fight against the Vikings?

Alfred, king of Wessex. Viking attacks on England began in AD 789 and by the AD 870s the raiders from Scandinavia controlled much of eastern England. Alfred won a victory at Edington in Wiltshire in AD 878, after which the Vikings made peace and agreed to stay within an area that became known as the Danelaw. Alfred was a wise ruler, and well deserved his title: Alfred the Great.

⬆ *The Vikings were explorers and traders, as well as fighters and looters. They travelled in 25-m longships, which held up to 60 men.*

Why were the Vikings so feared?

The Vikings were fierce fighters who arrived suddenly from the sea to raid towns and monasteries. They stole valuables but burnt books, for which they had no use. These bold sailors crossed the North Sea from Scandinavia to raid Britain, landing on beaches or rowing up rivers in their longships. Later, armies of Vikings ravaged the country. However, not all Vikings were bloodthirsty looters. Many brought their families to settle on farmland, or trade in towns such as Dublin and Jorvik (York).

⬅ *Irish and Viking warriors fought hand to hand at Clontarf.*

Characters in the legend include...

Guinevere	Arthur's queen
Merlin	A wizard and Arthur's counsellor
Lancelot of the Lake	The bravest of Arthur's knights
Sir Galahad	The 'perfect knight'
Sir Perceval	Knight who seeks the Holy Grail
Sir Mordred	Evil enemy of Arthur
Morgan le Fay	Arthur's half-sister
Uther Pendragon	Arthur's father
Ygerna	Arthur's mother

Key dates

407–410	Last Roman troops leave Britain. Saxons move in.
476	End of the Western Roman Empire.
503	Possible date of King Arthur's victory at Mount Badon.
582	Kingdom of Mercia founded in England.
597	Augustine arrives to preach Christianity to the English.
613	Northumbrians defeat Welsh Britons at Chester.
787	Vikings first land in England.
796	Death of Offa, great king of Mercia.
871	Alfred the Great becomes king of Wessex.
901	Edward the Elder recognized as King of all the English.
937	Athelstan is king of all Britain.
1016	Canute becomes king of England; he also rules Denmark and Norway.

The Middle Ages are the years between the ancient world (which ends with the collapse of the Roman Empire in the AD 400s) and the start of the modern world (roughly 1500). The early centuries of the millennium were years of war and conquest across much of Europe and Asia. Only the strong countries felt safe.

The name of Mongol leader Genghis Khan (c. 1162–1227) struck terror into those who feared his army might sweep down on them.

Who was Genghis Khan?

Of all the conquerors in history, few were more feared than 13th-century Mongol leader Genghis Khan, whose name means 'lord of all'. His horsemen conquered a vast empire stretching across Asia from China as far west as the Danube river in Europe. He destroyed cities and massacred thousands, yet under his rule trade prospered and all beliefs were tolerated.

What were the Crusades?

Wars for control of Jerusalem in the Holy Land, sacred to followers of three religions: Jews, Christians and Muslims. When the Turks prevented Christian pilgrims from visiting Jerusalem, the Pope called the First Crusade in 1096. Kings, soldiers, even children from all over Europe went on Crusade. There were eight Crusades in all, but the Crusaders failed to regain control of the Holy Land.

What was feudalism?

Feudalism was a social system based on land. The king owned most of the land, though the Church was also powerful. The king let out some land (called a fief) to a lord or baron, in return for soldiers when he needed them. The barons in turn let out land to lesser lords called knights – again in exchange for service. Peasants and serfs (poor people) only lived on the land in return for the work they did for their lord.

Medieval **mayhem**

Key **dates**

1001–02	Viking Leif Ericsson sails to North America
1066	Normans conquer England.
1096	First Crusade.
1206	Mongol chief, Temujin, is proclaimed Genghis Khan.
1249	Britain's first university at Oxford opens.
1265	First real parliament (De Montfort's) in England.
1270	Last Crusade.
1271	Marco Polo of Italy visits China.
1300s	First use of gunpowder and cannon in war.
1338	Hundred Years War between England and France begins (ends in 1453).
1368	Ming Dynasty begins in China.
1348	Black Death reaches England; Europe is hit with the disease.

The Bayeux Tapestry tells the story of the Norman Conquest of England in woven pictures. This section shows Norman knights on horseback and English foot-soldiers around the fatally wounded King Harold, struck in the eye by an arrow.

⬆ *Medieval peasants prepared the land for the next crop. In return for their work, they were protected by their lord.*

⬇ *Muslim and Christian soldiers fought in the Holy Land. It was not all fighting – each side learned more about the other's way of life.*

Why did the Normans invade England?

Duke William of Normandy led his army to England in 1066 after King Edward the Confessor died, believing that Edward had promised him the throne. The English, however, had chosen Harold Godwinson, a soldier, to be their king. The two rivals met in battle near Hastings in 1066. William won, and so became king: 'William the Conqueror'. The Normans, who spoke French, took over lands held by English nobles, and built stone castles to defend their conquest and prevent any rebellions.

⬇ *Norman soldiers landed at Pevensey in Sussex in 1066. Knights on horseback played a key part in the Battle of Hastings.*

Who signed Magna Carta?

England's King John. Magna Carta (the Great Charter) was a list of rights requested by angry barons, who felt that John was ruling badly. In 1215, they forced the king to put his seal to (sign) the Charter and promise to obey the rules within. Ever since, Magna Carta has been seen as a landmark in the development of modern government.

⬅ *King John signed Magna Carta at Runnymede, beside the River Thames.*

⬆ *Domesday Book was a survey of land-holding in England, drawn up in 1086 on the orders of William the Conqueror. No other record like it exists.*

Amazing **facts**

Mongol feats...

Genghis Khan led an army of 250,000 men and more than one million horses.

Heavy catapults for sieges were carried in sections on ox carts and put together.

Mongol soldiers lived on a diet of smoked sheepmeat and dried milk.

Soldiers were armed with bows, swords, axes and lances (long spears) with hooks for unseating enemy riders.

...and Norman knights

The 75-m long Bayeux Tapestry was probably made in England, not in France.

The Normans were descendants of Vikings who had settled in northern France.

Harold fought two battles in three weeks in 1066. He defeated a Norwegian army at Stamford Bridge, Yorkshire, on 25 September. Then on 14 October, Harold was defeated and killed by the invading Normans at Hastings.

The Norman knights charged into battle on horseback with long lances. The English fought on foot, with weapons such as axes.

People first reached North America 15,000–20,000 years ago, crossing a land bridge from Asia and travelling on foot and by boat. They gradually spread across the continent. The great civilizations of the Americas were in Central America (around Mexico) and in South America (in Peru), where people built large cities. Much of this culture was destroyed by Europeans in the 1500s.

⊙ *The people of Ancient Mexico built temples like this one at Teotihuacan, a city at its height in about AD 500, when about 200,000 people lived there.*

Who built pyramids in America?

Ancient peoples of Central America, such as the people of Teotihuacan and the Maya. The Maya were at their most powerful from about AD 200 to 900. They built cities such as Tikal (Guatemala) and huge pyramid-temples. A Maya city contained a tall pyramid-shaped temple in the centre, with special courts surrounding the temple, including ball courts for games. The Maya studied the Moon, Sun and stars, invented the first writing in America, and had a number system based on 20.

➔ *Machu Picchu was the Incas' last mountain stronghold in Peru. It was unknown to outsiders until rediscovered by an American archaeologist in 1911.*

When did 180 men conquer an empire?

When Francisco Pizarro of Spain led his men to conquer the Incas of Peru in 1532. The Spaniards found the Incas fighting a civil war. They captured the Inca ruler Atahualpa, and demanded a huge ransom in gold and silver. They then murdered Atahualpa and soon made themselves masters of the Inca empire, which stretched along most of the coast of the Pacific Ocean. The last Incas held out in the mountains in fortress towns.

Astonishing Aztecs

About the Aztecs
The Aztecs ruled their empire in Mexico from their capital city, Tenochtitlan, founded on an island in a lake in the 1300s

Religion was so important to the Aztecs that they went to war to capture prisoners to be sacrificed to the gods.

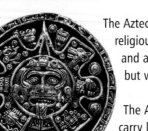

The Aztecs had two calendars: one for religious ceremonies, with 260 days, and another of 365 days, like ours, but with eight months, not 12.

The Aztecs did not use animals to carry loads or pull carts. They carried heavy loads on their backs or in canoes.

⊙ *This carving represents the Aztec view of creation – that the world had already been created and destroyed four times before the time of the Mayan era.*

The Aztecs' favourite war weapon was a wooden club studded with sharp pieces of obsidian (volcanic glass). The club was hard enough to knock an enemy out (to be taken prisoner) but not kill him.

⊙ *The serpent was one of 20 creatures that gave its name to a day on the Aztec farmers' calendar.*

Why did some Native Americans make human sacrifices?

Aztecs and some other peoples of Central America killed human victims to seek the favour of their gods. The Aztecs worshipped the Sun as the giver of life, and believed that unless they offered human victims to the Sun god their crops would fail. They thought that the hearts and blood of the victims served as food for the gods.

⬆ *A sacrificial stone knife used by Aztec priests to cut out the hearts of victims.*

⬆ *The Aztec warriors' clubs and spears were no match for Spanish steel, horses and muskets.*

What was the Aztecs' favourite game?

The Aztecs played a ball game rather like basketball. So did the Maya. The game was played in a walled court, which could be as large as 60 m long and was often next to a temple. Some historians believe the winners, not the losers, ended up being sacrificed to the gods – because they were the best!

➡ *The object of the game was to send a ball through a stone ring in the wall. Play was very fast and players were often injured during the match.*

Who was thought of as a god by the people he attacked?

Hernán Cortés, a Spanish soldier and explorer, who landed in Mexico in 1519. The Aztecs who lived there believed that the bearded Cortés was their god Quetzalcoatl, returned to them. Their calendar told them it was a special year and so they welcomed Cortés and his small army, though they were terrified of the Spaniards' guns and horses. Within two years, Cortés had conquered Mexico.

Key dates

1472 Aztecs at height of their power, after Tenochtitlan people conquer the rival city of Tlatelolco.

1502 Montezuma II became emperor.

1519 Cortés landed in Mexico from Cuba; Native Americans under Aztec rule rose against Montezuma and joined Cortés, who took Montezuma prisoner.

1520 Aztecs revolted against the Spanish; Montezuma was killed in the fighting.

1521 Spanish troops attacked Tenochtitlan and the new Aztec ruler Cuauhetmoc surrendered.

After 1521 Spanish conquerors destroyed Tenochtitlan and built a new city, now Mexico City.

➡ *Women made tortillas by hand and cooked them on a hot stone over a fire. The Aztecs called these cornmeal pancakes tlaxcalli.*

➡ *Aztec musicians played music on drums, conch shells and rattles while crowds would dance around them.*

This was an age of Renaissance – new ideas, discoveries, art and religious beliefs. European explorers set sail across the oceans, landing in America and also sailing around Africa to India and China. Art and science were changing, and so was people's approach to religion. The new ideas of the age changed the way people saw themselves and the world.

➔Columbus had three ships – the Santa Maria, Nina *and* Pinta. *Columbus persuaded King Ferdinand and Queen Isabella of Spain to pay for his voyage.*

Who won the Battle of Agincourt?

England's King Henry V won this battle in 1415 and claimed he was the rightful King of France. Henry led his army across the English channel and defeated a larger French army at Agincourt. The French king allowed Henry to marry his daughter and made him his heir. But Henry died in 1422, and never became king of both England and France. After his death, the English lost most of their gains in France.

Why was Columbus confused?

In 1492, Italian sailor Christopher Columbus believed he had reached Japan or China, when he had in fact discovered the 'New World'. Columbus had persuaded the King and Queen of Spain to finance a voyage to Asia, and his plan was to sail not east but west. Unfortunately, the map he had showed a very narrow sea, rather than the wide Atlantic Ocean, and it made no mention of America, which was unknown to geographers in Europe.

⬅French knights rode towards the small English army at Agincourt, only to be assailed by arrows from Henry V's archers.

Who was the Virgin Queen?

Elizabeth I, who became England's ruler in 1558. She was the daughter of King Henry VIII and his second wife, Anne Boleyn. Female rulers were expected to marry and many kings and princes stepped forward as potential husbands for Elizabeth. However, despite pressure from her ministers to marry and produce an heir to the throne, Elizabeth was reluctant to share her power and knew that marrying a foreign prince would make her unpopular. So she remained unmarried, and when she died in 1603, her Scottish nephew King James VI (1566–1605) became King James I of England.

Middle Age **miseries**

Disease, wars and punishments

The Middle Ages could be pretty grim. The Black Death killed about a quarter of Europe's population, and wars such as the Hundred Years War and the Crusades lasted on and off for hundreds of years. Argue with the Church or act like a witch, and you might be burnt at the stake. To see if someone was telling the truth, there were 'tests' – holding a red-hot iron bar or being thrown into a pond. No wonder outlaws took to the forest.

⬆Rats carried fleas…

➔…and fleas carried the Black Death germ.

Key **dates**

1450	Johannes Gutenberg invents printing with movable type.
1453	Turks capture Constantinople.
1487–88	Bartolomeu Dias of Portugal sails to the southern tip of Africa.
1492	Christopher Columbus sails from Spain to the Caribbean.
1497	Vasco da Gama of Portugal sails around Africa and on to India.
1499	Amerigo Vespucci sails to America, which is named after him.
1521	Cortés arrives from Cuba to conquer Mexico.

Who sent the Armada to England?

King Philip of Spain, who ruled over the most powerful country in Europe in the 1500s. Catholic Philip wanted to make Protestant England Catholic, too. In 1588, he organized a huge invasion fleet, called the Armada, to overthrow England's queen, Elizabeth I. The Armada was supposed to land a Spanish army in England, but it was attacked by the English navy and then driven north by storms. The great Armada failed.

Elizabeth I (1533–1603) gave her name to the Elizabethan Age.

Many Armada ships were wrecked on the long voyage home around Scotland and Ireland.

Who destroyed England's monasteries?

King Henry VIII, who reigned from 1509–47. Henry argued with the Pope in Rome over the issue of his divorce from his first wife (he married six times). The Catholic Church was facing Protestant 'reformers' who called for 'Reformation' – changes in the Church. Henry remained Catholic, but in order to get his divorce he made himself head of the Church in England, closing down the Catholic monasteries in England. Church lands were given to the king's supporters. Even so, Henry kept his title: 'Defender of the Faith', given him earlier by the Pope.

King Henry VIII's men, sent in by the king's minister Thomas Cromwell, looted monasteries in the 1530s and seized their treasures.

1519–22	Sebastian del Cano and survivors of Magellan's expedition complete first round-the-world voyage.
1533	Pizarro conquers Peru.
1534	Jacques Cartier discovers the St Lawrence River in Canada.
1543	Nicolaus Copernicus proves that the Earth goes around the Sun.
1577–80	Francis Drake sails around the world.
1577	Akbar the Great unifies northern India.
1582	Most of Europe changes to the new Gregorian calendar.
1590	Japan is united under the rule of Hideyoshi.

Amazing **facts**

Five ways of being killed in a siege…

Shot by an arrow/spear/crossbow bolt.

Falling off an assault ladder.

Scalded to death by boiling water or oil.

Having rocks dropped on your head.

Catching germs from a diseased corpse flung over the walls by an enemy catapult.

…and five painful punishments

Being burnt at the stake.

Having your ears or hands cut off.

Being dragged around town.

Sitting in the stocks and having rubbish thrown at you.

Whipping or hanging. Nobles could choose beheading instead, as it was considered a more dignified way to die.

Scientists used new technology to explore the wider universe and their new ideas were spread by the invention of printing. From 1700, the world entered an age of revolution, and political and economic change. By 1800, France had deposed its king, the American colonies had become the United States and the Industrial Revolution had begun.

➔ *Cook took with him scientists and artists to study and record the plants, animals and people of the Pacific lands.*

What caused the English Civil War?

The civil war in England was caused by a quarrel between King Charles I and his Parliament over royal power, religion and taxation. The war was fought between 1642 and 1651. The Parliamentary Army defeated the Royalists, and Charles was executed for treason in 1649. His son tried to regain the throne but was defeated in 1651, though he was eventually restored as King Charles II in 1660.

Where did Cook voyage?

James Cook (1728–79) was an English navigator who made three epic voyages to the Pacific Ocean. He explored the coasts of Australia and New Zealand, and reached the edges of Antarctica. Cook was killed by islanders in Hawaii.

When was London almost burnt down?

In 1666, when a fire in one of the city's old medieval buildings spread so rapidly that thousands of homes went up in flames. London had no proper firefighting service, so there was little people could do except run away, though attempts were made to blow-up houses to make a 'firebreak' so the fire would stop spreading.

◀ *In the Civil War battles, cavalry rode on horses, while foot-soldiers brandished long spear-like weapons called pikes.*

The age of **reason**

Key **dates**

1609 Galileo studies the Moon through his telescope.

1649 Charles I of England is executed, after a war with his own Parliament.

1667 Isaac Newton publishes the laws of gravity and motion.

1690 John Locke writes about democratic government.

1698 Thomas Savery invents the first steam-driven pump.

1768 James Cook sets out on the first of three Pacific voyages.

1701 Jethro Tull invents the first farming seed drill.

1709 Abraham Darby discovers how to produce iron cheaply.

1715 Louis XIV of France dies.

1776 American Declaration of Independence.

1782 James Watt makes the first efficient steam engine.

1783 American War of Independence ends.

1789 French Revolution begins.

Robert Winter

Christopher Wright

John Wright

Thomas Bates

Who was Clive of India?

Robert Clive commanded the British East India Company, which fought against French rivals in India during the 1700s. From 1600, English, Dutch and French merchants competed to control trade between Asia and Europe. As a result of Clive's victories during the conflict, the Mogul emperor of India lost much of his power to the East India Company, which ruled India until 1857.

⬆ *English redcoats fought Highlanders at Culloden, the last battle of the 1745–46 Jacobite rebellion.*

What was the Battle of Culloden?

Fought in April 1746, in Scotland, it was the last stand of Charles Edward Stuart or 'Bonnie Prince Charlie', to restore the Stuart monarchy in Britain. His Highland army attempted to overthrow King George II, but it was beaten by the English army, which had more men (9,000 against 5,000). Bonnie Prince Charlie fled into the hills before eventually escaping by ship to France. The Stuarts' hopes of regaining the throne had ended.

⬅ *War elephants were ridden during the Battle of Plassey in 1757, won by Clive and the East India Company army.*

Why did the Americans declare independence?

The American colonists were fed up with being taxed without having a say in the British Parliament. In 1775, Britain and its American colonists went to war. In 1776, during the war, the Americans declared themselves independent, creating the United States of America. With the help of the French, the Americans won the war in 1783, under the leadership of General George Washington, who was later elected President of the USA.

➡ *The Green Mountain Boys were American soldiers of the revolution, who captured the British fort on Lake Champlain.*

⬇ *The Gunpowder Plot of 1605 was a conspiracy by eight English Catholics to blow up the Houses of Parliament in London and kill King James I.*

Thomas Percy   Guy Fawkes   Robert Catesby

Thomas Winter

⬆ *Charles II (1630–85), who was restored to the throne in 1660, was known in Britain as the 'merry monarch'.*

⬆ *Louis XIV (1643–1715) of France built the Palace of Versailles to show off his wealth.*

The Sun King's legacy

In the 1600s, kings expected to get their own way. Charles I lost his head as a result. Charles II managed to survive, but his brother James II was forced off the throne because of his religious views. By the 1700s, it was clear a king could no longer ignore the wishes of Parliament and its people. In France, Louis XIV reigned longer than any French king, but refused to share his power with anyone. He also spent money lavishly and persecuted Protestants. People hated having to pay heavy taxes, and this resentment was one of the causes of the French Revolution (1789).

The Industrial Revolution was just one of several great changes in the 1800s. This was an age of factories, railways, steamships and fast-expanding cities in Europe and North America. European powers 'scrambled' to seize colonies in Africa, and the fast-growing United States became the youthful giant on the world scene. There were amazing advances in technology too.

What was the Industrial Revolution?

The Industrial Revolution was a great change that began in Britain in the mid 1700s. People began moving to towns to work in factories, inside which were new machines driven by water and steam. By the 1830s, steam railways were carrying raw materials, coal and finished goods to the new iron steamships in the docks.

↻ *During the Victorian era in Britain, many people moved from their rural homes to work in factories and live in houses close by.*

Who was Napoleon Bonaparte?

Napoleon (1769–1821) was an officer in the French army. Born on the island of Corsica, he was a supporter of the French Revolution and won many battles, though he failed to defeat the British with their strong navy. In 1799, he seized power in France, making himself emperor in 1804. He invaded Russia in 1812 but it was a disaster. Finally defeated in 1815, he died in exile six years later.

↑ *Napoleon was an infamous general, leading his army to conquer much of Europe.*

Why did Napoleon fight at Waterloo?

Napoleon's enemies joined forces to meet him at Waterloo (in Belgium) on 18 June 1815 after he had given up the French throne the year before.
He had left France for the island of Elba, but he was soon back, rallying his veteran soldiers for one last campaign. He was defeated by the combined armies of the English Duke of Wellington and the Prussian Marshal Blücher. He was exiled to the island of St Helena, in the Atlantic Ocean.

19th century **inventions**

Key **dates**

1804–05	Lewis and Clark map the West, to open the USA for settlers.
1805	Trafalgar – British fleet beats French and Spanish.
1815	Battle of Waterloo.
1827	First photograph, by Joseph Niepce, France.
1830	First passenger steam train in Britain.
1840	First stick-on postage stamps (Britain).
1854–56	Livingstone crosses Africa and sees the Victoria Falls.
1863	Battle of Gettysburg: Union army beats Confederates in American Civil War.
1864	Louis Pasteur discovers how to kill germs (pasteurization).
1869	Suez Canal opened.
1876	Telephone invented by Alexander Graham Bell.
1879	Electric light bulb invented by Thomas Edison.
1885	Karl Benz builds the first car.
1895	Marconi demonstrates wireless; first cinema films shown in Paris.

↑ *Alexander Graham Bell (1847–1922) pioneered the first telephone.*

Which war split the United States?

The American Civil War (1861–65), which was fought over the issue of slavery. The Northern states and President Abraham Lincoln, elected in 1860, opposed slavery. The Southern states wanted to keep black slaves to work on plantations and tried to break away, splitting the nation, and so began a bitter civil war. Five days after the war ended, Lincoln was assassinated.

Union (Northern) soldiers were called 'Yankees', Confederate (Southern) soldiers were known as 'Rebs'.

British troops fired on the advancing French during the Battle of Waterloo.

Custer and his men were outnumbered by the Native Americans, who won this battle. However, the Native Americans eventually lost the Indian Wars.

Where was Custer's last stand?

George Armstrong Custer (1839–76), made his last stand at the Battle of Little Bighorn in June 1876. From the 1840s, settlers headed west across America crossing the territories of the Plains Indians. The US Army was ordered to keep the peace and had to move tribes onto reservations. Some Native American leaders fought against this. General Custer, commander of the 7th Cavalry, split his force and led about 210 men against 2,000 Native Americans, mostly Sioux and Cheyenne, across Montana Territory. Custer and all his men were killed and the wars continued until the 1890s.

Sailing ships like this clipper were replaced by steamships, which could keep to regular schedules.

British rule lasted in India until 1947. British officials and their families moved to India during the period, which is now referred to as the Raj.

People headed for the goldfields of California, Australia and the Yukon to pan for gold, which would make them rich. However, few people made money through gold-panning.

Influential **people**

Florence Nightingale (1820–1910) – Nurse during the Crimean War (1854–56), who demanded changes in the way wounded soldiers were cared for.

Charles Darwin (1809–1882) – His theory of evolution in the 1850s was an explanation of why and how animals had 'evolved'.

Michael Faraday (1791–1867) – Faraday had little schooling, yet his research led to the development of the electric motor and generator.

Thomas Edison (1847–1931) – Edison was the brains behind the electrical revolution – the first light bulb and the first power station.

The 20th century saw two terrible world wars, an economic depression that brought unemployment to millions, and revolutions and fights for independence in countries ruled by colonial powers. It was the century of flight, of the cinema and television, of computers and traffic jams, of spaceflight and social change, equal rights and globalization – the spread of 'mass culture' to almost every country.

Why was the First World War the first modern war?

The First World War (1914–1918) was fought with new weapons that changed the nature of warfare. These weapons, such as artillery, machine guns, barbed wire, poison gas and aeroplanes meant that it was unlike any previous war. Millions of men got bogged down in trench warfare. In just one battle, the Somme (1916), more than one million soldiers were killed.

➔ *This huge artillery gun, nicknamed Big Bertha, was one of the weapons that made the First World War more terrible than previous wars.*

How did warfare develop after the First World War?

The Second World War (1939–45) was more costly than the first. Few countries escaped the fighting between the Allies and the German–Japanese forces. Aircraft dropped bombs on cities. There were new weapons, such as flying bombs and rockets, and finally the atomic bombs dropped on Japan in August 1945. Later in the 20th century, smaller wars were fought in Korea (1950–53), Vietnam (1957–75), the Middle East (1948, 1956, 1967, 1973) and the Gulf (1991, 2003).

What was the Great Depression?

The Great Depression was a financial crisis that struck the developed world in the 1930s. After the New York Stock Market 'crash' of 1929, banks and businesses closed and millions of people lost their jobs. Thousands of families lost their homes because they could not afford to pay the rent, and many people lost their savings. Panic spread to Europe, where factories laid off workers. The world's economies only started to recover from the late 1930s.

➔ *Jobless men marched from Jarrow in north-east England to London, to protest at unemployment during the Depression.*

A century of world wars

Warfare in the 20th century

The First World War (1914–18) was terrible but the Second World War (1939–45) was more costly. Few countries escaped the fighting between the Allies and the German–Japanese Axis forces. Aircraft dropped bombs on cities. There were new weapons, such as flying bombs and rockets, and finally the atomic bombs dropped on Japan in August 1945. Later in the 20th century, smaller wars were fought in Korea (1950–53), Vietnam (1957–75), the Middle East (1948, 1956, 1967, 1973) and the Gulf (1991, 2003).

➔ *The use of air power since the Second World War changed the way wars were fought and won.*

➔ *During the Second World War, people in Britain were issued with ration books like this one, which limited what they could buy each week.*

RATION BOOK

➔ *The German navy used submarines to sink supply ships travelling in convoys from the USA to Britain.*

Why was the United Nations set up?

The United Nations was set up in 1942 as a measure to resolve the terrible global conflict of the Second World War (1939–45). In the 1930s, a body called the League of Nations had failed to stop Germany's Adolf Hitler, and war had started. In 1945, leaders and representatives from 50 countries drew up the United Nations Charter at a meeting in San Francisco, USA. The charter was based on proposals made by China, Britain, the USA and the Soviet Union.

🔽 *Fifty countries signed the charter on 26 June 1945. Poland signed it shortly after, making the first 51 Member States of the UN.*

🔼 *Polish workers rallied behind the banner of their Solidarity trade union, which opposed the Communist government in the 1980s.*

What is Communism?

Communism is a social structure that, in theory, sets out to create a society of shared wealth and power. In 1917, a group of Communist rebels called the Bolsheviks turned imperial Russia into the Soviet Union. But by the late 1980s, Communism was failing. Factories were inefficient, people had little freedom and living standards were low. Many people wanted change, and across Eastern Europe Communist governments were removed. The Soviet Union broke up. Only China, Cuba and North Korea remain Communist.

What was the Cold War?

The Cold War was a time of suspicion between the USA and its allies, and the Soviet Union, China and other Communist countries. It began after the end of the Second World War in 1945. Each side distrusted the other, and each developed weapons of mass-destruction, such as hydrogen bombs. In the 1980s, more trade and the gradual collapse of Communism in most countries helped end the Cold War.

◀ *During the Cold War, both sides held huge stocks of missiles and nuclear warheads, such as this US Minuteman missile.*

Key **dates**

1903	First flight in an aeroplane by the Wright brothers (USA).	**1940**	Italy joins on Germany's side. France falls; Battle of Britain.
1909	Peary (USA) reaches the North Pole.	**1941**	Germany attacks Russia. Japan joins on Germany's side and attacks Pearl Harbor, Hawaii. USA joins war.
1911	Amundsen (Norway) reaches the South Pole.		
1914–18	The First World War is fought.	**1944**	D-Day invasion of France by the Allied armies.
1928	First antibiotic, penicillin, is discovered.	**1945**	Germany surrenders. USA drops two atomic bombs on Japan. Japan surrenders. UN charter signed.
1929	Wall Street Crash in New York.		
1930	Rise of Nazis in Germany.	**1947**	Pakistan is independent from India.
1936	First TV broadcast in Britain.	**1953**	Hillary and Tenzing climb Everest.
1939	Germany invades Poland; The Second World War begins.	**1957**	First space satellite, *Sputnik I* (USSR).
		1961	Yuri Gagarin (Russian) circles the Earth in the *Vostok 1* spacecraft.

1968	Soviet troops crush freedom movement in Czechoslovakia.
1969	US astronauts Neil Armstrong and Buzz Aldrin land on the Moon.
1975	End of Vietnam War.
1989	Collapse of the Berlin Wall in Germany, and end of Communism in Eastern Germany. Tiananmen Square demonstration in China.
1991	Break up of the Soviet Union, and the first Gulf War.
1994	First free elections in South Africa.
2001	September 11 tragedy in the USA.
2002	War in Afghanistan.
2003	The second Gulf War.

Why not test your knowledge on world history! Try answering these questions to find out how much you know about ancient empires, battles and wars, kings and queens, explorers, conquerors, inventors and much more. Questions are grouped into the subject areas covered within the pages of this book. See how much you remember and discover how much more you can learn.

Ancient Peoples

1 What is a long barrow?
2 What name was given to Celtic priests?
3 Odin was the chief god of which race of people?

Ancient Empires

4 Which empire was conquered by Pizarro?
5 For what is an abacus used?
6 In which year were the very first Olympic Games held: 776 BC, AD 776 or AD 1000?

7 Which ancient civilization worshipped gods called Isis, Osiris and Horus?

Ancient Egypt

8 What did the ancient Egyptians use to sweeten food before the discovery of sugar?
9 Which material was accidentally made by ancient Egyptians when they lit a fire on a beach?
10 Was the Egyptian pharaoh Tutankhamun buried in a pyramid?

Ancient China and India

11 Of which people was Genghis Khan a war leader?
12 Where was the empire ruled by Akbar the Great?
13 Which major world religion was founded by the Indian Prince Gautama?

14 Who fought in the arenas of ancient Rome?

Ancient Greece

15 Which Greek philosopher founded the Academy in Athens?
16 The Greeks invented which type of government?
17 Athena was goddess of what?

Ancient Rome

18 With which Egyptian queen did Julius Caesar and Mark Antony fall in love?
19 What name did Octavius take when he first became Roman Emperor?
20 What was the Colosseum in Rome used for?

Ancient Britain

21 In which year did the Romans successfully invade Britain?
22 About when did the Iron Age begin: 19,000 BC, 1900 BC or 190 BC?
23 Which female East Anglian leader rebelled against Roman rule in Britain in AD 122?

After the Romans

24 The Battle of Hastings is recorded in which famous tapestry?

25 Who is the only English king called 'the Great'?

26 Which country was ruled by Kenneth MacAlpine in the AD 840s?

The Middle Ages

27 Which prince led the English to victory at Crécy in 1346?

28 King Richard I of England fought in which foreign wars?

29 What were the Crusades?

Ancient America

30 To where did a Viking named Leif Ericsson sail?

31 Which explorer, who discovered America, sailed in the *Santa Maria*?

32 What sort of structures did the Incas build to worship their Gods?

1400–1600 Age of Discovery

33 What was the name of the first fleet sent by Spain against England in 1588?

34 Which English king was killed at the Battle of Bosworth in 1485?

35 Which English king did Anne of Cleves and Anne Boleyn marry?

1600–1800 Age of Revolution

36 At which battle did the Indians defeat General Custer?

37 A group of English Catholics conspired to blow-up which London building in 1605?

38 Which explorer was killed by islanders in Hawaii?

1800–1900 Empire and Industry

39 Which industry was revolutionized by the invention of the flying shuttle: weaving, transport or mining?

40 What did a man named Dunlop invent in the 1880s?

41 Who commanded the British fleet at the Battle of Trafalgar in 1805?

42 Fidel Castro was president of which communist country?

The Modern World

43 What was special about the Heinkel He-178 plane, first flown in 1939?

44 By what nickname was American astronaut Edwin Aldrin known?

45 With what is the inventor Charles Babbage linked: computers, medicine or balloons?

Answers

1 A kind of Stone Age grave
2 Druids
3 Vikings, or Norsemen
4 Inca empire
5 Mathematical calculations
6 776 BC
7 Egyptians
8 Honey
9 Glass
10 No, he was buried in a tomb
11 The Mongols
12 India

13 Buddhism
14 Gladiators
15 Plato
16 Democracy
17 Wisdom
18 Cleopatra
19 Augustus
20 Gladiator games
21 AD 43
22 1900 BC
23 Boudicca
24 The Bayeux Tapestry

25 Alfred the Great
26 Scotland
27 The Black Prince
28 The Crusades
29 Religious wars against the Turks
30 North America
31 Christopher Columbus
32 Pyramids or ziggurats
33 The Armada
34 King Richard III
35 King Henry VIII
36 Battle of Little Bighorn

37 Houses of Parliament
38 Captain James Cook
39 Weaving
40 The air-filled tyre
41 Nelson
42 Cuba
43 It was the first jet plane to fly
44 Buzz
45 Computers

The publishers would like to thank the following artists who have contributed to this book:
Richard Berridge, Steve Caldwell, Vanessa Card, Peter Dennis, Nicholas Forder, Terry Gabbey, Luigi Galante,
Alan Hancocks, Sally Holmes, Richard Hook, John James, Kevin Maddison, Janos Marffy, Angus McBride,
Terry Riley, Pete Roberts, Martin Sanders, Peter Sarson, Rob Sheffield, Graham Sumber, Rudi Vizi, Mike White

All photographs are from:
Corel